Blockchain

The Ultimate Guide to Understanding Blockchain Technology, Fintech, Bitcoin, and Other Cryptocurrencies.

Anthony Tu

information contained within this document, including, but not limited to, —errors, omissions, or inaccuracies

For more information, go to

www.wonpublications.com

Table of Content

About the Author

Anthony Tu (also known as Anthony Tuanga) is a computer scientist, author and a cryptocurrency investor. He has been working in the field of computer science for the last 10 years and completed his degree at Harvard University. He came across cryptocurrencies early in 2011 and fell in love with the technology.

He is a large investor in cryptocurrencies such as Bitcoin, Ethereum and continues to share his vast knowledge in the space.

Outside of work, he is a family man. He loves to spend time with his beautiful wife and son.

Introduction

I want to thank you for choosing and purchasing this book, *'Blockchain: The Ultimate Guide to Understanding Blockchain Technology, Fintech, Bitcoin, and Other Cryptocurrencies.'* In this book you'll find everything you need to know about Blockchain, from the fundamentals of Blockchain Technology, to the nitty gritty side of Blockchain implications on industries. This book will be your ultimate guide and something you can refer to now, and also in the future. As a BONUS, not only is this book about the essentials of Blockchain Technology, information about other Cryptocurrencies will be added for your benefit.

Bitcoin, Ethereum, Litecoin... What do these cryptocurrencies have in common? Besides being a money magnet in modern investing, they're all based off the same technology. Not only these 3, but ALL cryptocurrencies are based off the Blockchain Technology. Blockchain Technology has come under mass adoption in recent years, with the growth of the famed Bitcoin, the blockchain has been implemented in different industries, primarily within Fintech, the financial industry. It has been used to track records, payments, processes, and today, you'll learn how one of the most underrated revolutions in technology is going to change our future.

I know you are excited to learn about the Blockchain, and we'll get started in a second. Again, I'd like to thank you for choosing this book. I have comprised everything I know about Blockchain in my years of experience, and I know you'll enjoy this book. This is the beginning of your cryptocurrency adventure and I hope you're as excited as I am.

For More information, check out www.wonpublications.com

Let's get started!

Chapter 1: What is the Blockchain?

Before we get into depths of blockchain technology, we must understand what is the blockchain? The honest truth is that you can't really answer this question without telling you how blockchain works because blockchain is one of those few items that is explained through how it works rather than what it is. A lot of people consider it much like an accounting ledger, or for non-accountants, like a file cabinet full of files of information. However, the biggest difference is that it is online, and the fact that it is open source, meaning anyone can access the information at any given time.

How a List Works

To begin understanding blockchain, we first need to cover how we formulate a list, like a 'To-Do' list. Most of us will go through the items that we think we might need, or cover all of the items in our selected area. But let's say that the list we're going to work with within this first chapter is a grocery list. In a grocery list, you will either have the individual who will specifically think about what items are needed before they ever write the list and then they will check to make sure their assumptions are right. The second individual will look over the different items in the fridge in comparison to an initial list that will instruct the writer of that list on what they should be checking in order to formulate a list upon what is missing.

In both cases, both individuals will need a prior list in which to check against in order to form a new list based off of the list that has been checked and insert anything that is missing into the new list. This is generally how a list works but in most programming languages this is not called a list, but an array. An array is a list of items that you first put into the list and in programming terms, we would form a first array that holds all the possible items that we want to check for inside of our fridge. Then we would develop a second array of all the items that are currently in our fridge. Finally, we would write a step-by-step process, otherwise known as an algorithm, to check the items in our first array to compare it to the items in the second array to create or generate a third array that will contain all the missing items inside of our fridge. This is how the computer views a list inside of the digitized world and so it is this first step that truly makes up the core logic of what blockchain is and, essentially, how it works.

How an Encrypted List Works

Let us first go over the first form of encryption that any encryption enthusiasts learn about whenever they begin studying encryption. This is known as the rotation 13 technique, and what it basically means is that you take a letter such as 'A' and you rotate through the alphabet until you get to the 13th place after what 'A' stands for. This, in our case, would be the letter 'M' because it comes 13 places after the letter 'A'. This is the most basic form of encryption on the planet and it was actually developed by Caesar, the emperor of Rome. The way that we would normally encrypt the list is pretty similar to this technique but we rely on the computer to develop a random system that will generate a random string of characters (a word), special characters such as an '!' or '?', numbers, and other such items that you can input via a keyboard. This computer-generated random string would essentially be what is known as our key.

Our key allows us to take the information in our list and encrypt it with an encryption technique that utilizes the random string and the numbers or letters inside of the word in the array to jumble the actual meaning of those words. The technique is usually far more advanced than rotation 13 but you can think of it as a technique that's usually very similar to how rotation 13 works but in a less predictable manner. Therefore, we have something known as a public key. This public key allows us to decrypt the information inside of the array. This is actually quite simple and very easy to understand. It's not really practical whenever you're trying to get users to interact with each other because you may have a public key, but that doesn't mean much if everybody else has a public key. If both individuals have public keys it essentially means they can see the same material that you are seeing. Keep in mind if no one else has your public key so no one else can see the material. This is when things get a little bit more complicated.

How a Shared Encrypted List Works

This is when we begin evolving our concept of the list into a much more complicated schema. When a shared list is encrypted, each individual is given a public key and the server has its own private key. The private key may be generated with a separate string of randomness that is stored as part of the information itself but since all of the information is encrypted, finding out where the private key is inside of the information becomes almost impossible to predict. It becomes even more difficult to predict if you decide to use random string sizes but this is far more complex to develop for a system that is going to be used on a shared network. Now that you have your private key attached to the information and you have your public key, you can then share your public key with the person that you want to know about the information on the list so that they can use the public key to enact the private key that will then decrypt the data that we have been encrypting. This is how a shared list works and it's actually something that has been implemented for a very long time but has never been conceptualized like a blockchain. Instead, this technology has been hidden away inside of something called a 'session'. Whenever you go to a website, you are then subjected to a flood of different types of code whether the person shows Java or python to run their back in script and then how much CSS or HTML, I'm not going to get into any of that. However, sessions are built inside of JavaScript and it is because cookies became so insecure on JavaScript that sessions were developed. A cookie cannot be encrypted unless you manually encrypt it yourself and so it is much more difficult to handle private information via a cookie. However, sessions provided a secondary form of this and what would happen is that the key that is private would be generated every two weeks and the key that is public would be stored on your computer in your cookie. Therefore, instead of needing to constantly login when you were away from the site, you only need to just make sure that you had your public key and that you were in the time frame of the current private key. This would provide a type of session where you would be able to interact with website during the time that these keys were available. However, once those two weeks were up, the public key and the private key would be regenerated so that any bad guys couldn't figure out the information if they wanted to.

This is what Blockchain is

All of this has been to build up the explanation of what blockchain is and give a general idea of how it works but we will get into the specifics in the next chapter. However, we will go over the conceptualized idea of how blockchain works here, and that is to say that a blockchain is a shared list but on a global scale with a key component that helps ensure the validity of the keys on the network. You see, encrypted currency has the problem of the double spending issue. Double spending refers to the fact that digital information can be copied and pasted and so in the past when you wanted to do something like digital currency, not a lot of people understood that the digital currency could literally be copied and pasted and then used twice within the same network even though it would normally be seen as not a valid transaction. It was the definition of digital fraud. Before digital fraud existed, these things included things like identification and paperback money. Therefore, in order to achieve an encrypted currency you would need to solve the double spending problem. To solve this problem, everybody had to have the list of groceries, as it were, so that they could figure out which Keys had transactions at which times. This was to show that the owner of those keys is not, or is the person doing the transaction. By having the network solve the problem of 'who' currently has those keys, you can effectively stop the double spending problem but you need a way for those transactions to be delayed so that the network, everyone in the network, has the opportunity to validate a transaction. This is where the concept of proof of work comes in which will be covered in the next chapter.

Chapter 2: How Blockchain Works

Everyone Downloads the Encrypted List

In the first step of the process, people who receive this encrypted currency will download the list of everybody who has a portion of the same encrypted currency along with their private keys. The way that this list is generated is that you have a worker bot that receives a name and that name is used on the front end, the back end or the middle of the encrypted string that represents the digital currency. Now keep in mind that a blockchain doesn't just have to be utilized inside of currency because one of the key aspects of a blockchain is that it can be utilized with anything that represents digital information, and not just currency. This is actually why this book has been created because a lot of people hear blockchain and then also associate that with Bitcoin, but Bitcoin is just the beginning. So, everyone has to download a list of all the worker bots and their encrypted strings to develop the first array that we were talking about. This is going to be the list that everyone utilizes in order to check whether a person or, rather, a worker bought is the owner of a certain encrypted string. This essentially means everyone is responsible and accountable for the blockchain.

A Transaction Request is Made

Now that everybody has a list of all the currencies on the network as well as everyone who actually owns that currency, they can begin to make transactions on the network, and this is when the second part of our blockchain comes into action. When the network detects that a transaction request has been made, it then sends out a signal to everybody who has currency on the network that also has a current working miner on the network. These worker Bots, which are called miners, then receive the transaction request and receive a block of code that they are going to solve but the problem is that everyone needs to have a chance of solving this block of code and if you have a machine that is capable of solving the block of code faster than everyone else then you run into the problem of falsifying that block of code. Essentially, it is logically possible for an individual to create a network setup that sends a bunch of positive results throughout the network saying that the transaction is valid. But the point of everyone solving the problem is that everyone has a chance to provide an answer from an untampered list. Depending on how many people validate the transaction that is occurring, the transaction will either occur or be denied based on this number of positive results.

The number of random people that are chosen to solve the current transaction problem must be different people on the network that have an equal amount of time to solve the problem. This is based on the power of the network so that the transaction is more secure. This is because if the most powerful device on the planet could be the only person or machine that's validating this transaction, then you invite the shadow powers of the government. Essentially, it would ruin the purpose of an encrypted currency before the encrypted currency ever got out. Therefore, the only two factors that ever provide a confidence level of security in the blockchain are the methods of encryption and how many individuals validate the transaction trying to make its way through the network. The more individuals that can test and validate a transaction the more secure a network will be because it means that there are less people who are capable of fooling the system. The problem is that the system has to figure out a problem that will take everyone around an even amount of time in order to figure out.

A Problem is Determined

Therefore, the very first step in our blockchain encrypted currency beyond dispersing the currency itself and then detecting a transaction request is determining how the transaction will be validated by other users. In order to delay the transaction time so that everyone has an even opportunity to solve a problem, the proof of work concept was developed as a concept that would utilize a delay timer and gauge the difficulty of the problem generated based on the computing power of the network. Keeping in mind, the main purpose of blockchain technology is decentralization, so having a system where everyone works together is key. Therefore, in this order, the problem is generated. A transaction request is made and so the entire network receives a confirmation that the network has received a transaction request. The entire network then utilizes an algorithm to test how much power is on the entire network in terms of computing resources. Once the entire network has generated the difficulty level of the problem that needs to be solved, the problem is then generated so that it takes a specific amount of time for a portion of that computing power to solve it. Once the problem has been generated, the system then chooses a random amount of individuals on the network that will then attempt to use their computing power to break down the problem and solve it. If the computers on the network can solve it during the allotted time then they send a proof of work to the entire network to show the entire network that they have solved the problem and thus the work is validated and by having the work be validated you also have the transaction be validated. The only problem is that if the estimated problem is too difficult for the network or if the network is unable to solve the problem then either the network judged the difficulty too harshly or the transaction is invalid. In most cases, the transaction is valid and it will go through but in the special case that it judged the computing power to be too much then it will repeat the process with a significantly lowered difficulty so that it can validate that it was just the computing power that it misread rather than the validation of the transaction itself. Either way, the network responds to the network with a successful completion or two red flags that suggest that someone on the network not being entirely truthful. If the network responds with positive feedback then the transaction goes through otherwise the transaction is blocked from happening.

A Problem is Solved

However, it's not entirely reasonable to expect everybody just to donate their computer power in order to handle these transactions because the more computing power that the network has, the more security that it has. So the network needs the computing power, but people who have the computing power don't actually need the network. This creates a problem of incentivizing the people on the network to actually do this type of work and this is where the value of solving the transaction comes into play, and why Bitcoin had such a huge impact on cryptocurrencies that we know of. Whenever somebody would get the proof of work problem from the Bitcoin Network, the people who solved the problem would then be able to receive a reward for solving the problem in the first place, and that was usually represented as the transaction fee of the transaction request. The transaction fee was so small that it was almost nonsensical to say that it was unfair in some sort of a way because it was often pennies on the amount that you were trying to transfer. The point of getting into this transaction validation game was to constantly run these machines so that they could solve the problems faster, and faster but this creates a problem with the network because the network judges the computing power of the network in order to generate the problems. So the faster that you actually try to solve the problems, the more difficult the problems get on the network and so it kind of created this self-ending loop where Bitcoin will eventually reach a computing necessity that is far out of the reach of the average individual, or even the Farms that are built specifically to harness this transaction receiving power.

Chapter 3: The Difference Between Blockchain and Bitcoin

What Bitcoin actually is

The reason why most people see the blockchain and Bitcoin as the same machine is because Bitcoin is actually built on the blockchain. The problem is that the Bitcoin machine is not necessary for the blockchain technology to be useful. You see, blockchain can work without Bitcoin because almost everything that I just described could be handled with items such as cars or anything that you really needed to trade on this network. The only problem is that the proof-of-work concept relied on the computing power that the network could provide, and since this was a self-inflicting problem on the network, eventually the proof of work concept would exhaust the network of the necessity to validate the transactions.

A Bitcoin is a randomized string of letters and numbers that represents a personally held value that the people of the Bitcoin Network back with their own concept of value. This is not that different from how the actual monetary system works because a dollar used to represent how much gold used to represent. Gold represented a specific type of Rarity in the world and since a material was seen as rare, it was utilized to represent the end goal of *work value* in the world. However, the United States dollar is no longer based off of what we would call the gold standard, and it is simply based on what we think it is worth in a new form of money, known as Fiat money.

The only difference between Bitcoin and actual money is that bitcoin's value is determined by the users on the network without any influence of any type of special body. Fiat money is often determined by both the users on the network, as well as the organization that is in control of printing that money. A perfect case in example is the Chinese monetary system. They are controlling the value of the Chinese Yuan by inflating the worth of their Chinese monetary system, and then deflating it to reap the rewards of making something very expensive or very cheap for other people to buy. This is a very sly and dirty trick that some countries use to conquer other countries without the necessity of an army.

Why the Proof-of-Work

Many people often ask why the proof-of-work concept was the concept that was utilized to help solve the double spending problem but it really boils down to being the first concept in the market in the first place. There are several renditions of this type of concept, and Bitcoin's proof of work simply was the most popular because Bitcoin was the most popular at the time, and still is today. Additionally, Bitcoins were handed out as incentives and were virtually free in the beginning before they started to take on value by being traded and utilized as a form of currency. What the proof-of-work concept did was allow enough time for multiple nodes in the network to solve a problem that involved validating their list of individuals who were currently on the network with those coins being transferred to other accounts on the network. This allowed for the nodes on the network to be chosen randomly, the problem to be chosen randomly, the solutions to be chosen randomly, and the delay time to be chosen randomly. If you haven't noticed by now, the security of this network is based on how random it can possibly be, and so the proof-of-work concept allowed the network to be almost as random as you could possibly be when it came to validating transactions and handling multiple users on the same network.

The Blockchain and Proof-of-Work Problem

As we've already discussed, the blockchain doesn't work well with the proof of work concept because the proof-of-work concept relies on the overall power of the network itself. This creates a recursive problem where the network gets more powerful as the network exists and continues to grow. The more the network continues to grow, the more difficult the problems gets to solve and so this ultimately slows down the entire progress of the network just so that transaction can be validated. This means that the network can eventually become insecure because the longer it takes for computers to validate the transaction request, the more time is allowed for bad individuals to insert their own code so as to falsify the transactions on the network. Therefore, if you can somehow find the open source code to figure out how to predict where the transaction request validations are going to be sent to. You can intercept those requests and then also provide falsified data for those same requests. This allows people to cheat the network at its own game because the network is taking too long to provide the needed transaction validations on the network. This means that, overtime, the network will eventually get so complex at the problems that it generates, that it will eventually crumble underneath its own weight. The proof-of-work concept is really a self-destructive principle that was built into the blockchain without really thinking that the blockchain would become this popular. That's really what it boils down to. The only reason why this problem exists in the first place is that this person who created Bitcoin didn't think that Bitcoin would become as massive as it is now, and it is probably the reason why Bitcoin amount will only ever reach a couple million coins. Now, a lot of people think that a couple million coins is not a lot in terms of money but you also have to realize that these are whole coins we are talking about. If you were to talk about the fraction of the coins, which can go down into trillions, then you are talking about a currency that can literally surpass the amount of money that is going through the United States dollar system. Therefore, you have millions of Bitcoins in which each 1 coin can be broken down into trillions of cents.

The Replacement for Proof-of-Work

There are actually several theories out right now that propose to replace the need for the proof of work. The primary waste that comes with proof-of-work is the amount of electricity that is required in order to do the calculations provided by the computers. Since the amount of electricity that is utilized to do these calculations have begun to reach such a scale that it could require as much power as it requires to power all of Denmark, the necessity of replacing proof of work becomes quite vital for environmental reasons.

Proof-of-Space

One of the concepts is the proof-of-space, and it essentially is another delay tactic that says that a hard drive has a certain amount of space at a certain time. The reason why this is another delay tactic is because a hard drive takes a certain speed in order to read information from it and so when you talk about the space of a hard drive, you talk about how much time it actually takes to calculate the space in a hard drive. This would basically store the numerical version of space that you have left, or you have, on a hard drive where your last cryptocurrency existed. This would serve as the test for the proof-of-work concept. Instead of relying on computing power to solve some massive complicated problem, you would have to guess at the amount of space that the person who is transferring the coin had at the time that they received the coin. Needless to say, this is a theory that is a work in progress.

Proof-of-Time

The second concept that is currently in the works is the proof-of-time concept. This concept is a guess at what time an individual would have received a certain coin. Essentially, a computer would go through all of the different listings of those coins that are available to everyone in the network, and try to guess which coin is their coin based upon time. This would take enormous amount of time simply because the many people on the network really determine how long the algorithm would take. Essentially, you have the amount of people on the network X how many coins are available on the network itself. As you can see, that would be a massive number that would take a lot of computer power to figure out which coin was the coin that is being transferred over the network. Additionally, this type of calculation would also need to guess the exact date that the network detected and when that person received the coin. So you have the combination of the amount of people on the network X the amount of coins that are in the network, and this is then X by how many dates are possible from the creation of the network. Needless to say, it is a different type of mathematical problem but it is so massive that it would take quite a while for a computer to figure out but since it is a simplistic problem to figure out. On the bright side, you wouldn't need the amount of high-power hardware that is currently relied upon in the proof-of-work concept.

Proof-of-Stake

The last section of the concepts that are currently out there to replace the proof-of-work concept, is the proof-of-stake concept, and this is provided by the Etherium network. The developers of this cryptocurrency saw that many people are going to be owning this form of cryptocurrency, and wanted to provide a simplistic solution to the proof-of-work concept. You can simply switch over to how much stake you have inside of the network. This meant that you had a certain amount of coins and you had to prove that you had a certain amount of coins in the network. You prove this by viewing transactions of how many coins that the person was transferring. This relies on something called a lookup table, which is to say that it takes an enormous amount of time to look up information on a table, and the challenging part is that no matter how much power your processing core has, it will generally take the same amount of time to look up the information. Even if you have a processing power that has 8 cores to it, you still have to solve the problem in the same speed as many other people in the network. Needless to say, all of these are very complex in their implementation. None of these have been tested on a very big network, and so the last concept, the proof-of-stake, is a concept that is going to be tested out by one of the big alternative cryptocurrencies. Whether the concept will be better than the proof-of-work is not entirely sure, but the mathematics say that such concepts *might* be better.

Chapter 4: The Benefits of using Blockchain Technology

No Bankers

Perhaps the first real benefit of using blockchain technology is that we get rid of those shady bankers that like to charge us useless fees for unnecessary work. There are so many different fees that are charged by Bankers that don't actually have a good reason to be a charge. I'll just let you know I'll use this time for a miniature rant. I apologize in advance. I mean, really, we have a charge simply for having an account with a company? What brilliant villain thought up the idea that we should charge our customers for being our customers? The insane idea that you must pay a monthly fee in order to hold your money inside of a bank account is absolutely absurd, especially when you know that you can go to a checking account held by a credit union and get one for absolutely free most of the time. I mean, seriously?! What person charges their customer for doing business with them? Then you have your transaction fee. Transaction fees are mind boggling when you understand why these are useless charges. In the old days, a transaction fee would normally require a bank to take a person from their labor force and denote a certain amount of money needing to go to another bank. There was a physical transfer of money between banks in order to validate a bank transfer. This is the reason why things like checks took a couple of days because they had to validate that the amount existed in the first place. When we switched to things like credit cards and debit cards, this validation process became almost instantaneous and didn't require anyone to go anywhere to do anything. All it required was some digital numbers to be changed from one account and then changed to another account. The possibility of physical cash has almost evaporated from the monetary environment, and to charge people to transfer digital numbers that don't require any physical cash behind it is absurd. The bank doesn't have that kind of cash inside of it in the first place, it represents just how crazy banks have gotten with their useless charges.

The invention of PayPal was actually to help solve the problem of why it took so long for money to be transferred between two companies when it could be done digitally. A blockchain utilized with currency has already shown that you can completely remove a banker from the equation by transferring all of your money into the cryptocurrency that you believe in and then utilizing the cryptocurrency as real money. There is no need for the banks to hold the money because all the money is in your hard drive or in somebody's hard drive online. It is heavily encrypted, making it safe so that no one can break into it. We might talk about wallets, we might not, but the point is that Bitcoin has already shown that you don't actually need Bankers in order to complete transactions with money anymore. In the past, Bankers were needed because we all needed a place to safely store our money. For instance, a billionaire does not want to have a billion dollars lying around their house because it is quite obvious that somebody's going to try and break in and steal it. Therefore, a banker was needed in order to store that amount of money in a very highly safe manner so that the billionaire could literally feel at peace with where their money was. Since cryptocurrency is digital, you can store it on a hard drive and since the coins themselves only take up a few kilobytes of information, it doesn't take much space to store the amount of money that you have. This completely removes the necessity of needing a bank in the first place because you can be your own bank again like the days before we created the monetary system.

Real Online Car Buying

There is a rather big problem when it comes to buying cars because the car industry is famous for making it rather difficult to buy a car in first place. For instance, how is a person supposed to buy a car without a car in the first place? How exactly do you get to the place that you need to be at when there are specific locations that dealerships can and cannot be to buy a car? You kind of need a car to get a car. Now, unlike Banks, the reasons why you have to be at a physical location in order to purchase a car and basically go through a week of red tape is kind of reasonable.

The first thing that buying a car means is that you are now becoming part of the population who utilize the roads that the government works on in order for you to actually drive on those roads. In order to actually provide the amount of money that's needed in order to keep up maintenance on those roads. It is understandable to first register your car and then to also tag your car so that each person can donate towards the entire system that helps keep our roads working. This is kind of understandable. The fees for this are actually relatively low in the comparison charts for the past because I remember that nearly 5 years ago I was paying around $60 to $70 and, this year, I paid around $35 to drive my car around. It's actually gone down over time because the maintenance amount is not as high as it once was. With that being said, you also have to keep track of the cars on the roads to make sure that if someone were to steal your car, then you could have proof that it was your car in the first place. You also have to validate the transaction, and finally you have to have insurance on the car most the time. Now if you notice, there's actually no need to go to a dealership but why do they make you go to a dealership? Well the truth of the matter is that you first need to be able to physically see the car itself before you purchase it so that you can validate that the car exists. Well, a blockchain could easily handle this because the entire system is about validating information and if all the cars on the network are cars that are being bought and sold by people on the network, then the information should be valid. The car manufacturers could generate the information about the cars into the system before they are placed on the market. The second step in the process is that you need to provide proof that the car is actually yours, and since the entire blockchain is about being a validity system, then the car would be underneath a system that could prove that the car is yours. Therefore, you have the option to purchase a car that you know exists because it can't be on the network if it doesn't exist, you are able to provide proof that the car is yours because it's on the network in the first place, and you are able to prove that you are purchasing it by simply making a transaction for the car in the first place. All three of these steps make it possible to purchase cars online without having to go to a physical location, like every other product in the world.

Government Red Tape Thinning

Think about how many jobs inside of the government are complex because they need a form of validating that something occurred. You need a bookkeeper in order to validate that transactions occurred inside of a government entity, you need a notary to confirm that transactions of a physical type occurred within a government entity, and the list really goes on to comprise most of the United States government and other governments. The truth is that most of the government's size is due to the amount of validation that the government has to do to make sure that facts are facts. We have an entire IRS for this purpose alone. The appalling nature behind all of these mechanisms needed to validate something that should naturally be true makes one open their eyes whenever they look at the inner workings of their government. A blockchain would remove almost all of these jobs because a blockchain would keep track of any financial tracking that you would need to keep track of. It would keep track of all of your physical transactions because you would only need to upload that information into the network once and then make a transaction of that over the network. Most of the jobs that require any type of transaction validation or validation of existence can simply be done by the blockchain. That doesn't mean that the government will fully rely on it because it is technology, and technology ultimately always has some type of hole in it but since most of everything is digital nowadays, it's kind of foolish to not rely on something like this.

Power to the Users

With a blockchain, the power is finally back in the user's hand. In order to understand this, we have to go back to how we originally began trading things. You would have something that I wanted, and so I would try to find out what you wanted so that I could trade you for what I wanted. Needless to say, this was difficult to manage whenever you had large societies and so the natural solution was to trade in materials for something that represented the amount of work that went into an item. When we switched from using our materials as money to paper or coin as money, we lost control of the monetary system. The monetary system was now in the control of whoever was printing or making the currencies for that system. With a blockchain, we are generating the currency for the system and so the users of the system now have control of the system. Needless to say, most companies that are built on a scheme where they have control of the monetary system don't like the idea of no longer being a business and this means that the Federal Reserve is heavily against the idea of a blockchain based currency. This is because the power will be returned to the users because we are generating it, and we determine its value. Why is this important? If you remember correctly, the gold standard was the only time where the user had most of the control over the monetary value that they owned. When we switched from the gold standard, something set in stone, to the fiat money that we have now. We gave control over the monetary value to the Federal Reserve. During the gold standard time, we had a ton of growth and expansion, but as we've had the fiat money, we have slowly degraded over the years. During the gold standard, we determined our own worth, while the fiat money has allowed others to determine what we are worth.

Chapter 5: The Disadvantages of using Blockchain Technology

A Shadow Currency

The chief concern that comes with cryptocurrencies and the slapstick concern that comes from people who benefit from the fall of cryptocurrencies is the fact that some cryptocurrencies can be manipulated by organizations behind the creation of the cryptocurrency. If someone were to create a cryptocurrency that was sufficient in the job of a cryptocurrency and it had an exploitable hole that could allow an individual to manipulate the process behind the crypto-currency, then you could effectively build a cryptocurrency that can be controlled by others rather than the decentralized cryptocurrency that we all know and love. This would effectively be the conspiracy level of regular money but in the form of cryptocurrency, because instead of a giant organization controlling all of the money in the world, you would have the original creators controlling the money on a cryptocurrency market and deciding who should get money and who shouldn't. This isn't that big of a deal, simply because many people would be able to switch over to different currency networks but it would take a vast amount of money in order to do this if you invested a lot of time in this cryptocurrency network.

Performance

The current problem that we see with most of the cryptocurrency networks is that the performance of the technology it seems to not be able to handle scale very well. This is actually a common problem with the technology world in general because most technology is built for local use and scalability is usually an afterthought until it becomes a problem. A good example of this are websites that are specifically built around handling social media networks. They aren't capable of handling a very large scale. We saw incidences with companies like Twitter, and Myspace, whenever they gained users in the millions and weren't able to take on the load very well. The same thing can happen in a blockchain if you have a method that requires a delay of time before other transactions can happen. Let's say that no other transactions can happen at the same time as your transaction. What happens if you have trillions of transactions coming after your transaction? Are you ever going to be able to get a transaction in? This is the primary concern around performance inside of cryptocurrencies.

Lack of Regulation

While many people love to propagate the fact that the network of cryptocurrencies are not regulated, that is a crutch of the network of cryptocurrencies. A lot of people simply don't trust an automated system because unless the people who are validators have people who validate the validators, then you don't have a chain of responsibility. Therefore, if a network were to be hacked, who exactly is going to stop them? This system is designed to run automatically without the need for a primary figurehead to ensure that everything is running because that is what it means to be decentralized. Essentially, if such a system were to be hacked then you have the problem of who would assume responsibility for taking care of that problem. The same cannot be said about current fiat monetary systems because these monetary systems have their governments held accountable for what happens in the monetary system as well as the corporations who control the influence of money. Since everything is run and operated by the user, it would be the users on the network who would have the responsibility of fixing the network. The problem is that it is the users on the network who may have caused the problem and so the cause of the problem is not often the solution of the problem. As you can see, this... creates a problem.

Massive Energy

We are already seeing this with the proof-of-work concept because whenever you take the solution for validating a transaction to the much higher scale of working with billions of people, you run into the problem of power consumption. Right now, the problem with Bitcoin is that it takes too much power to run the systems needed to validate the network. If you based your system on the amount of power one could generate, you have based yourself on a limited resource because there is only so much power that can be dedicated in the world.

Refusal of Adoption

This is actually a problem that we are currently seeing in certain countries that refused to accept cryptocurrencies. The current cryptocurrency markets are heavily volatile for some countries and these are new technology to these countries that it's simply not worth their time to risk the venture inside of these cryptocurrencies. Therefore, if you cannot get a country to accept the currency then that currency is devalued by the rejection of the currency in a country. A lot of people think that currency is localized and it's worth is determined locally but the reason why the United States dollar is worth so much right now is because it can be used in almost all countries. Cryptocurrencies are not that well trusted yet and so a lot of countries have either put limitations on them or bans. This is because they don't want a type of currency that they cannot control inside of their own country and so the amount of places that you can use a currency also ultimately decides how much a currency is worth.

Maintenance of the Network

When I talk about the maintenance of a network, most people think that I'm talking about a labor force that actually takes care of the network physically. The truth of the matter is that the labor force behind most cryptocurrencies are the people who decided that they wanted to create it in the first place. Normally, they won't stop taking care of it unless they see that it's gone past the point of no recovery. No, instead, what I'm talking about is who is going to take over when there is no more incentive to maintain the network? When you talk about concepts like proof-of-space, proof-of-time, or proof-of-work, you have a network that is dedicated to validating the transactions on the network and so that means that those computers on the network are what maintain the network itself. What's to say that the network will simply see a lot of people cash in their Bitcoins or their cryptocurrencies and just leave the network? What happens when all of that computing power is gone? This is a massive underlying problem with things like cryptocurrency because the worth of the network is ultimately decided by how many people use the network. This problem has the potential to lose trillions of dollars if the industry gets big enough.

If you're enjoying this book, please leave a review on Amazon ☺.

Don't forget to check out the previous books. Check out the Author's profile, Anthony Tu, for more information,

www.wonpublications.com

Chapter 6: Blockchain and the Financial Industry

A Stable Currency

If we have learned anything about our different monetary systems between countries, they're almost always organized by very shady individuals. Let's take the Federal Reserve in this case because there is a lot of hate for the Federal Reserve because of how they handled the issue in 2008. The Federal Reserve reacted to the situation by printing out a ton of money to save people who should essentially be saving our money in the first place. The problem with this is that it sent the entire country into a recession because all of the real estate that was bought during that time simply became worthless because no one had any money to buy any of the real estate and everybody owed money to the banks.

When you have an organization capable of deciding how much money should be released into the market, you have an organization that is capable of making a very horrible decision like the Federal Reserve. Whether the horrible decision was actually a horrible decision or not is up to the philosophers that handle financial transactions but the truth of the matter is that this conversation wouldn't exist inside of a blockchain. This is because the blockchain only deals in what is currently in the market and feeds the market at a very specified rate. This would create the very first fully stable currency that heavily relied upon user activity rather than promises. You might think this is weird but let's go through how your credit card handles the money in your account. It is a known fact that you can run up credit cards and then just not pay them unless you owe close to hundreds of thousands of dollars. It is simply not worth the money to hire a lawyer to go after you when you only owe a couple thousand dollars. It is more money to pay the lawyer then it is to go after you and so most of the time the credit card companies will wait until you actually achieve debts of over hundreds of thousands of dollars where it would be a profitable venture to go after you with a lawyer. Having said that, where does the credit card company get its money? The money itself is nonexistent. The money is money that everyone else is paying into the system and so what happens is that the credit card system is so large that banks are okay with accepting promises for money. Essentially, the bank is okay with accepting an IOU from MasterCard and Visa where the money is going to be transferred into the bank account over a period of time. You can actually set something like this up with your existing bank but you have to have the same amount of credibility as these two massive credit card issuers. Within a blockchain, this is not possible and so defaulting on money is not possible in side of this network. Let me restate that, you cannot default on the money in the network because you cannot spend money that you don't have in the network. Governments that are currently in trouble financially are often in trouble because they spent money that they don't have and now they don't have a way to pay it back and so other countries that rely on said money are fearful of that country might default on the amount of money that they owe. You cannot do this with a blockchain.

Instant Transactions

When you transfer something over a bank to another bank, the transfer is not immediate. It may seem like the transfer is immediate but the truth is that the transfer could take quite some time. What happens is that the company (that's charging you the fee for the items that you have) has sent a digital request to the banking system that you have to see if your account currently has the amount of money needed to purchase that item. Your bank sends an affirmative or a denial based on how much money you digitally have at the time. This does not include things like bills that are coming in or pending requests. With a blockchain, such a request is not required because everything is transferred almost instantaneously to the point where you have a split-second where the money is in the network and then the money is in the account. Once a request has been made with a bank, the digital representation of that money is transferred. That doesn't mean that the money is inside the other person's pocket. What it means is that the bank currently believes that you have that money digitally and the other person got that money digitally. On a physical level, it could literally take a month for that money to transfer into the next Bank. However, for convenience value, you are allowed to make such transactions digitally because all the banks control the monetary system and have agreed that this is a good idea. If a bank were to fail when you made a transaction and the bank itself was to no longer be in business, all of the money inside of your bank would be invalid and so what happens if you made a last-minute transaction that said that you had the money but your bank didn't pay up? Would you owe that company money? These questions don't need to be asked with a blockchain because the blockchain is self-representative and self-validating.

Chapter 7: Blockchain and Other Industries

Financial Records

Pretty much any industry that is involved with keeping track of financial records would be practically useless provided that there was a system that could keep track of the different cryptocurrencies coming in and out. Since everything would be digital, you could easily just set up automated machines to do the work for you and you would just need a developer for that. Since most companies have developers on their staff or can hire a freelance developer, there would be almost no need for positions like bookkeeping and tax experts because you could simply just submit your records via automatic mail and the receiving end would automatically judge what type of taxation you would need as well as what taxes needed to be applied. The entire process would be almost automatic except for setting it up.

New Industries Previously Non-Digital

A lot of problems that arises when it comes to validation is the need for enormous purchases to be non-digital because digital can be falsified. This includes things like buying houses, cars, or anything that costs more than $1,000. If we were to utilize blockchain technology in its full capacity, then all of these industries that were previously not digital would dramatically change because of the rare possibility that an item can be falsified would automatically switch over to a digital version of themselves because the blockchain is self-validating. This would take a process like buying a house, which normally takes almost half of a year depending on what house you're buying, and turns it into an almost instantaneous transaction and all of the different variables such as registering your home, seeing how many people live in your home, and all the different variables that your government keeps track of would be instantly changed whenever that house became yours because all of that information is in your account.

Advanced Mathematics

A lot of people avoid the industry of mathematics but the truth is that the industry of mathematics is vitally important for every functioning device that we have on this planet and yet one of the most boring. When you remove the enormous jobs from the market that require steps for validating transactions, you will have likely removed nearly half of the jobs on the market. The new massive job market would be job markets based around mathematics and since programming, game development, and cryptocurrency development are all centered around mathematics then you would likely have a huge influx of new individuals who seek a higher education when it comes to mathematical theories and the mathematical Sciences.

Court Systems

A lot of the problems inside of the court system industry could actually be solved by the blockchain solution because one of the biggest courts in the court system is the financial court. This is where people argue about how much they spend or how much is fraud in the system or how much they actually did not pay the IRS. In these cases, court rulings would not take weeks to months to even years as they normally take because the blockchain could easily prove the path that the cryptocurrencies took. The only problem would be backtracking where the currencies are in the Market along with where they came from. One of the inventions that the current cryptocurrency market hasn't provided is a back tracking system that allows you to track where the money came from. Since automatic bookkeeping would become a reality for all cryptocurrencies, these issues could be readily solved.

Chapter 8: Ethereum and Other Cryptocurrencies

Here are some examples of different types of cryptocurrencies,

Bitcoin Cash (BCH)

This cryptocurrency still utilizes the information of the Bitcoin blockchain prior to August 1st 2017, but it became its own coin after that date. It's creation occurred because there was a disagreement about how Bitcoin could become faster and this coin represents the side that wanted to make it faster by making the transaction faster.

BitConnect (BCC)

This cryptocurrency already utilizes Proof-of-Stake as well as Proof-of-Work. It is the lending version of the Bitcoin.

BitShares (BTS)

This type of coin is meant for trading in cryptocurrencies, but refuses all forms of current fiat money. This is to preserve the anonymity of the user. The value of the network is due to the fact that it ties cryptocurrency value to objectifiable forms of assets like BitGold, which represents the cryptocurrency of the gold standard.

Bytecoin (BCN)

Bytecoin's sole concern is ensuring crypto-users stay crypto-users and are never identified by anyone via a digital trail. It purposely hides the details of the transactions to keep the transaction valid but hides the users.

Dash (DASH)

This is an Altcoin that is tied to providing better privacy, low transaction fees and transaction times than Bitcoin. There's nothing else that makes this coin special.

Dogecoin (DOGE)

Don't worry, it started off as a joke but it is currently a serious cryptocurrency because it was treated like an internet meme and is one of the top coins. The name is actually designed to rebuke the status the Silk Road gave to Bitcoin and it is based heavily on Litecoin.

Ethereum (ETH)

Ethereum is currently very popular because it extends upon the idea of blockchain further than Bitcoin. It is the most common platform for initial coin offerings (ICO), meaning new coins that are created generally use the Ethereum network.

Chapter 9: Impact of Blockchain Technology

One Step Further Towards a Global Market

One of the big problems when it comes to fiat money is that every civilization has their own form of money. The European Euro, the United States dollar, the Japanese Yen, and so on and so forth. Every single region has their own type of money but with something like Bitcoin or another cryptocurrency, you remove the country's ability to produce their own monetary system. By removing their ability to produce their own monetary system, you remove their incentive to stay isolated from the global community. For instance, the United States government would not normally deal with countries that have no legitimate monetary value to them unless there was a humanity right or need in that section that the United States government felt they needed to step in for. If that country had the same currency as the United States government, the United States government could easily push money over to that country in cryptocurrency rather than physically pushing themselves onto those countries so that they can help. The Chinese market would not be trying to inflate and deflate their current currency to control the flow of currency coming in and out of the United States and other countries. There are several reasons why it's a good thing to move towards a global market rather than individual markets working together.

Further Growth in Rare Areas of the Technology Industry

If we continue to invest in cryptocurrencies, we will see a massive spike in the amount of people that are interested in working in those industries. When is the last time that you met an individual that said they worked in cryptology? Last time I checked, I only met one inside of a movie. I know that this may make it sound like some funny joke that I meant to say but the truth is that this is the truth. The last time I actually saw a cryptologist in person was inside of a documentary about cryptologists. It's kind of horrible to say that that is how I met a cryptologist. Keep in mind that these cryptology industries help protect the information that you're actually going to be using on a daily basis and is the reason why your society is currently functioning in the monetary world, in the cellular world, and in other facets where a connection to the internet is required. These people are crazy important but they are so rare that it takes a documentary to see one unless you happen to be a lucky individual that somehow met one. This is a technology industry that people don't go for as much as things like web development, database management, and other more popular themes because that's not where the money's at, plainly put. A person who is capable of developing a cryptocurrency network has had an opportunity like never before because understanding encryption and being able to improve upon current encryption is what a cryptologist is supposed to do, that's why they are hired. The more encryption that's out there, the more that people will be interested in studying. Then you have areas like online banking, online banking protocol management, and similar almost never heard of fields that are specialized by people who have been in their jobs for decades and that if they die, we have a serious problem. Needless to say, this is kind of a good thing for these areas as it increases the incentive to be a part of them.

A Power Behind Improving Computers

One thing that has definitely stagnated throughout all of the industries is that there hasn't been much of an incentive to improve upon computer design. Most of what powered the computer design era was the ever-present need for better graphics but as we reach the potential maximum for what we can recognize as better graphics, we are making very slow, incremental improvements to our processing techniques and Hardware. Something unique that happened because of cryptocurrency was that graphics card companies began specializing their graphics cards to handle the specific load of cryptocurrency enthusiasm. These customers were after big graphics cards that could handle a lot of calculations at lower wattages. When you look at the average PC Master race gamer, you will not find an individual who is overly concerned about the amount of wattage that their system is using. So long as the wattage amount is no more than a thousand Watts, most Gamers simply don't care about how much power their systems are using and so you had beefy graphics cards like the GTX Titan that sucked up a monstrous amount of electricity in order to provide the amount of quality that the game or needed. It wasn't about efficiency, it was about how much graphical power the graphics card could deliver. What happened when you reached the cryptographic cards is that the companies began to care about the cryptocurrency customers and develop a graphics card that was very high power but at very low wattage. With the GTX Titan you needed a max of 600W and it supplied 2688 cores. With the recently released GTX 1080Ti, you have the same power withdraw but with 3584 cores. You might think that is simply because of how old the GTX Titan was, but the previous version of 1080, the regular 1080, only came with 2560 cores with only a gain of 100W back in your pocket. This represents the fact that the Nvidia company realized that people who were mass buying their product wanted something that was not only powerful but also something that could offset the wattage required to perform their cryptocurrency mining. Therefore, this represents a direct Hardware representation of how the computer industry tried to change to accommodate these specialized customers. Additionally, many people have seen variant releases of mainstream gamer graphics cards that have better stats because they are built for mining and so these variant cards either provide a lower core count with a significant drop in wattage usage or a higher core count with a slightly increased wattage usage. On top of that, a lot of the new graphics cards are coming in kits that are specifically designed to sell towards miners rather than Gamers because they either sell them in bulk for much cheaper as part of a selection of graphics cards that the company pre-selected to sell towards cryptocurrency miners or they provided an incentive for cryptocurrency miners to purchase those graphics cards so that the mainstream could have access to the singular graphics cards. The reason why they did that is because they know that the mainstream graphics card buyer will likely only by a single graphics card whereas the cryptocurrency miner is probably going to buy several.

A Sign of the New Generation of Technology

Before cryptocurrency really took off, encryption was not on the mind of a lot of individuals and a lot of the concepts that cryptocurrency tackles were also not on the mind of individuals. Sure, things like lessening government control was definitely on the minds before but that's pretty much always been on the minds. Instead, things like transaction security and how to lower the cost of gaming, how to make computer hardware more environmentally friendly, and things of this nature were not truly considered an important part in the technology industry up until the massive influx of cryptocurrency miners. I believe that the current sleuth of changes that are happening inside of the technology industry in the financial industry because of these cryptocurrencies is because it is a sign of the next step in the evolution of our technology and we are just experiencing the beginning motion of this evolution as we try to secure cryptocurrency into our world as a permanent form of currency that everyone uses. I believe that cryptocurrency is going to be the new version of money and that many of our jobs are going to be replaced by jobs that are based inside of technology. This is simply a sign that all of this is going to occur.

Conclusion

Welcome to the end of this book and I wanted to leave off on a topic that a lot of people are interested in because they are unsure as to whether the Bitcoin is worth investing in or if the blockchain is really as useful as people make it out to be. I want to tell you that Bitcoin is likely going to die. Bitcoin was the very first form of cryptocurrency and it was not developed to handle the amount of scale that it is currently handling. The fact that Bitcoin has already sprouted up at least four offshoots of its own brand should represent the fact that Bitcoin has some severe problems. That being said, investing in Bitcoin may or may not be a good idea because Bitcoin does make changes over time and it's really up to the future as to whether investing in Bitcoin is a really good idea. This is kind of how markets work and how stock markets work so you should have expected the standard response when it came to investing but the honest truth is that cryptocurrencies have a lot of room to grow. There is a huge market that wants the benefits of cryptocurrency. When there is a market that wants a product then you know that product is going to grow even though the market may seem a little shaky at first. However, that doesn't compare to what blockchain can do because it is a methodology that can be used throughout several industries. A lot of people think that the fate of blockchain technology is tied to Bitcoin or some other cryptocurrency, but the truth of the matter is that it is tied to the people who develop your technology. Unless you are a developer, you have no control over whether blockchain becomes a standard practice in the industry or if blockchain is going to change the world because it is a tool that already exists and it is up to the developers of our technology to utilize that tool or to not utilize that tool. Let me tell you that the developer community really likes the idea of the blockchain and while there is some criticism behind it, most of everybody agrees that this is going to be a tool that is commonly used inside of the industry.

I hope you received valuable from this book, if you enjoyed this book, please leave a review on Amazon.com. Any review is greatly appreciated and I would like to thank you again for choosing this book. I strive to do the best I can and constantly revise the content.

Actions to Take

Once again, congratulations! Now that you're an expert in Bitcoin, it's time to master the other coins. This diverse knowledge will not only benefit you as an individual but enhance your investing abilities. By now you also know Bitcoin is the largest coin in the cryptocurrency market, but did you know that close second is a cryptocurrency by the name of 'Ethereum'?

Ethereum is the leading platform developer of ICO's (Initial Coin Offering). This means that most coins that are newly released are operated on the Ethereum network, approximately 75% of total coins released. This uncapped potential has seen Ethereum has seen an explosion in value in the course of 2017, from $8 in January to $300 in October. Find out why!

If you want to know more about the leading cryptocurrency platform developr, check out my other book, *'Mastering Ethereum: The Ultimate guide for Beginners to Understanding Ethereum Technology, Ethereum Investing, Ehereum Mining and Other Cryptocurrencies.'*

Master the second largest cryptocurrency today!
You can find this on the Kindle store;
ASIN: B076W27PT6

Did you know the difference between a 1% and 3% fee can reduce your return on investment by half? This is because over time, the *compounding* of those fees dramatically reduces your profits. Sometimes it's not the price of the asset that matters but the fees that make a huge impact.

Here's a snip of the book.

Exchange 1:   BTC/USD: $3500 + Fees: 3.99% = $3639.65

Exchange 2: BTC/USD: $3550   +   Fees: 0.99%   = $3585.145

As you can see above, exchange 1 prior to fees presents a more attractive investment than exchange 2. After the fees, exchange 1 is clearly more expensive.

These expert tips will help you reduce uncertainty and allow you to maximize your profits. If you would like to know more about cryptocurrency investing, check out my previous book, '*Cryptocurrency: 5 Expert Secrets for Beginners: Investing into Bitcoin, Ethereum and Litecoin*'. In this book I cover all the basics of cryptocurrencies and essential information experts use when they invest begin to invest into cryptocurrencies.

You can find this on the Kindle store;

ASIN: B07571MSY5

www.ingramcontent.com/pod-product-compliance
Lightning Source LLC
Chambersburg PA
CBHW070131240526
45468CB00002BA/905